Electrical Theories of Femininity

Sarah Mangold

Also by Sarah Mangold

Household Mechanics, selected for the New Issues Poetry Prize

Chapbooks:
The Goddess Can Be Recognized By Her Step
I Meant To Be Transparent
An Antenna Called the Body
Cupcake Royale
Parlor
Boxer Rebellion
Picture Of the Basket
Blood Substitutes

Electrical Theories
of Femininity

3 9082 13010 5904

Electrical Theories of Femininity

© 2015 Sarah Mangold

www.blackradishbooks.com

First printing 2015 in the United States of America

Cover Design: Jared Hayes

Cover Image: Brian Dettmer, *Integrated Electronics*, 2008, Altered Book, 11" x 10" x 8⅛". Image courtesy of the artist. www.briandettmer.com

Thank you to the editors and publishers of the following journals, chapbooks, and anthologies where many of these poems first appeared:

Action Yes, American Letters & Commentary, Aufgabe, BlazeVOX, c_L, Court Green, Dusie, Fact-Simile, Handsome, Horse Less Review, Little Red Leaves, No Tell Motel, Poetry Northwest, Puerto del Sol, Rattapallax blog, the Toronto Quarterly, Web Conjunctions; An Antenna Called the Body (Little Red Leaves, Textile Series, 2011), I Meant To Be Transparent (LRL e-editions, 2012), Parlor (Dusie Kollektiv, 2007 & reprinted by above/ground press, 2013); Building is a Process / Light is an Element: essays and excursions for Myung Mi Kim, (P-Queue/Queue Books, eds. Michael Cross and Andrew Rippeon, 2008), *PRESS: Activism & The Avant-Garde*, (Wheelhouse, ed. David Wolach, 2009).

This project is supported in part by an award from the National Endowment for the Arts.

ISBN 978-0-9850837-8-6
LC 2015931600

Contents

I meant to be transparent	5
Dismantling imperialist nostalgia	7
Color as corruption	8
Everything is a side issue	9
An equally deedy female	10
Public inscriptions are all around us	12
She has a gilt complex and a poison pen	13
Tell her I'm giving up thinking in words	14
Complaints about the language she inherits always there	15
I expected pioneers	16
The three areas of technical understanding— photography, persistence of vision, projection	17
Since the beginning	20
Drilling is thrilling	21
Didn't anyone tell you how to gracefully disappear in a room	22
The book made an emotion of the lost territory	23
The Machine Has Not Destroyed the Promise	27
Spencer Enjoyed Relaxations	28
Spencer Asks, There is No Answer	29
The Women Saints as Poets	30
Monstrous Sense and Sight	32
From What Are Phenomena Rescued	33
How Information Lost Its Body	34
Mothers Must Always Prove Their Readiness	35
Your Point of View into Account	36
Electrical Theories of Femininity	37
Pataphysical Nebraska	38
Phenomena in the Overtone Services	40
Bred to Domestic Affection	41
Happened as I Know it Happened	43
Custodians of a Fractious Country	44

Setting the Landscape in Motion	46
The Study of Individual Points	47
Roofer to the Principal	48
And What is True of Landscape is True of Everything That Can be Filmed	49
Enthusiasms and Execrations	50
Technique Without Explication	51

The Panic of the Multiple Narrative World	55
An Antenna Called the Body	56
Harassed Cotton Operatives	57
At Once in Solemn Compulsion	58
Neither Sonorous Charm nor Originality of Meaning	59
Every Man a Signal Tower	60
Feeling Is an Episode in Self-Production	61
A Temporary Aberration of Female Productivity Purpled in Depravation	62
Proof of Good Faith	63
Meeting Your Trapdoor	64
A Face to Meet the Faces that You Meet	65
The Formula of Imitation Aims at Representation	66
Sinking the Only Swimming Pool in Venice	67
The Realm of the Dead Is as Extensive as the Storage and Transmission Capabilities of a Given Culture	68
Outside of Praise and Precision	69
What It Means to Write the Early History of Anything	70
How to Electrify Human Hands	71
Plumb at the Center of Rejoicing	72
The First Thing the Typewriter Did Was Provide Evidence of Itself	73
Wax-Cylinder Recordings of People Threatened with Extinction	74
The Dropping Of a Demon Down the Chimney	75

for Paul

I meant to be transparent

    Things were astounding enough
        the passenger ferry   the steeple
            enough to make you die of astonishment
        an empty river
        the swimming bench   tips of trees   to take wing
          if you did nothing at all

I like that feeling right next to the stillness   being alive   if one could
could realize that clearly enough

If I don't eat there's a situation   what everyone did was just
a distraction from astonishment
        magistrate building
      sitting neatly as adults   the body as message

I appreciate a riot   let the hand down   revering books and language
      charm   amulet
        I preach practicality as a vision of the future
      pilgrim   saint
        I am not John Dewey

The shrine of the *beyond   that is within*   sideways next to the imagination   one must remember it is there   fluid   Sometimes miracles were written on parchment   twisted into a paw abracadabra   shining in the pocket of a good realist   to agree the minutes are a modifier

An emphasis falls on silhouettes
      trenches   lilies
      substituting for an original body and voice   you recall treatments of nothingness   *books were not stories printed on paper they were people   the real people*   silence was pictorial again

Dismantling imperialist nostalgia

She finds the woman who wrote searing scenes. A rosy linoleum making a shapely thing of a chance meeting with a stranger. Fantastic titles surround. It was monstrous to break in. Wildness. Consciously shining as if she won knocking out any particular or blindered soirée. Making havoc and complications. Two tall Ts looking from face to face. Claiming audience and suggestions for accommodations. As everyone was the moment. Community crowned one for the other. Hearing only form is a kind of perfect happiness. Pancakes and pajamas. Science as cosmic scandalmongering.

Color as corruption

But when you threaten to go about labeled gingerale for ladies
only the problem is like certain businesses   You use the wrong
expressions

     perversions

     depravities

     horrors

Ugliness   rooms wherein the eye finds neither food nor rest
    Estrangement
         perpetuating claims   cultural visions
Keeping the center clear   the walls a pale soft shade   space and
perspective created by her treatment of the corners

Making a far distance there
         bearing vertical stripes
         of rare indefinitely retreating blue
To attend to color then is a part to attend to the limbs
of language—whatever you have on ice—as a theater of
simultaneous possibilities—Does the beautiful girl act as creator
thief or scribe—Whether they are not glad to have escaped
the bob fringed art-surge lodgings—sheltering their first five
weeks—there is constant action and the action is in us

Everything is a side issue

    She is backwards and forwards in a sense of time as vertical
        rather than horizontal
            Traveling the difficulties   no one had ever said
        fabric about anything

                The arrival of a dedicated afternoon
a dangerous looseness   and of the guests prune-and-prism
behavior instead signals the time to perform another reading of the
paragraph just read

Pirouetting elegantly about one must both read by ear and follow
the sound
read by eye
        cakes
            eyebrows perpetually up

    To make the reader strange to herself for her swift
    perceptions   longing for participation
        his eyelids had oftened served as shutters

            An action and a process
            nothing there   *butterfly*

An equally deedy female

> She gathered up the scattered sheets
> a non-geometrical attempt to supply information
>
> about what was far and what was important
> bringing it down into life
>
> and illustrating its operation
> there was good
>
> it was more like an expressionist portrait
> than an identification photo
>
> Perhaps this was a turning point
> leaving panic behind
>
> It was for sinners not navigators
> these cupboards full of ranged freshly-labeled bottles
>
> the distance from Oberland to Jerusalem
> a ruler across a map
>
> Drawers of stored materials
> newly sorted and listed
>
> turned each way and each way is undone
> the multitude of charts and the many accounts

affect and atmosphere

the presentation so annotated and tabulated

Her successor would relievedly find herself

the sport and spectator of fueled efforts

The world

of a super humanly deedy female

canaled

and could be lived up to

Public inscriptions are all around us

She recalled the general pleasantness of the atmospheres during those last moments before she became for them a kind of monster—To refuse to return to the next—*she was a misfit in domestic service*—a crisis of expectations

She should have been a grenadier or a countess—Insert immanence through the hall to answer the door—It was found he had access to money—*She was a procession— humanity in disdainful movement*—unassuming right and left contemplation—A world of people going into space— and at any moment might have the bad manners to go up in flames—Heels out between us—almost enough to make dangerous a fantastic intensification of everyday people

A hundred song magazines in order to make people attend— Love is a lavish language—Love is a huntress song—To his philosophy of astonishingness a bill of goods—*The astonishingness of doors opening when you push them*—It was going to be this sweater—She had spoken firmly from the context of her private speculations—Lots of big big revolution behind my eyes—one long moment of attention

She has a gilt complex and a poison pen

The night was like a moment added to the day. Signing his name and forgetting his friends   like years going backwards to the beginning of ambient textuality.

Endless couplets and in the brilliant sunshine the unchanging things began again. Non-pressure modalities. The characters of the story were always tiresome. The administrative and problematic heavy industry publications.

The ideas   the wonderful quotations   if you looked closely   metadata containers   everybody knew. I'm reading a novel   I'm on an architectural space. *Dear Eve   Shakespeare is a sound.*

He was secretly interested in adventurers and adventuresses the book in durational energy. Paid for does it make dinner an uncomfortable domestic container. *Before she finished the chapter Miriam knew the position of each piece of furniture.*

The information on the surface was romantic and modular. Every page a discrete unit absorbed in a massive amount of footnotes.

Tell her I'm giving up thinking in words

As a witness of enormities   the failure that underlines the modernists. Regardless of street   a perverse way of making Americans   by making him realize something of the enchantment. A long gramophone recording over time that for him was just a way of being charming.

To take someone who doesn't want the pleasure of language and as desirably remote from science. Or when they've found perfection beaten   vocabulary I don't have access to anymore.

Everybody is a special category. Without an infant do not feel obligated. Concluding that you don't want to risk electrocution they spoke English to each other.   Erasing patterns of assimilation. One must   you know   keep one's metaphors up-to-date.

Complaints about the language she inherits always there

        Years ago he said there will be no more him and her
            the novels of the future will be clear of all that
                Farewell my red balloon
                    romance is solitary and permanent
                    Need #1 in everybody
                      hinges
                      calculable
                        White walls
aluminum   the smell of fruit A tangle of nerve-racking heavy industries   Gather a feeling but not an exact picture   How they all had handles   Our point is now transparent   Destroying everybody teeth first

I expected pioneers

        The door is off its hinges. What people forget about the avant-
        garde forwards and backwards. The Pre-Raphaelites wanted
        to bring the background forward. The tyranny of perspective
        they wanted all views at once   two poles to the rickshaw.
        To be taken together seriously picked

                              sweet

                              cola

nicely every gesture has a sound shape. Make a drawing
of the sound.
A dynamic space not a linear space

            performative

            crushed

the condition of fury. There is an absorption of the minor
character   as porous as everyone   seems an enormous amount.
The bonus round nothing with butter. Swell   certainly your
desire. Not *about* anyone. She wanted her poem to go somewhere
to be leaving the house.

The three areas of technical understanding—photography, persistence of vision, projection

> *Till now she had reached to where perhaps feeling fades into thought*—her whole being a torch peevishly seeking inflammable material—Create foreground—reenact and place the miracle behind the surface—Miscarried inspirations of a prospective audience too long kept waiting—the continuous performance going on behind all invitations—To focus upon this or that of the film itself—short circuiting in a frivolous world—Dwelling behind all invitations I tried to make her admit—punctuality in the coming through of the hidden shape of things is scientific evidence—and a little dangerous—and apt to be pathological

Why do these scientific people suppose that something supplying hints when you are not looking for them—hints that overpower the voices of reason and common sense are more strange and mysterious than anything else—Collective seeing—small ceremonial prepared for a group—*Perhaps scientific people are intellectual saints and martyrs sacrificed to usefulness*—believing that men and women are taught from the beginning to speak "his"

And I waited for his arrival—Those people who hail taxis and dismiss servants with one imperious gesture—*The torment of all novels is what is left out*—Slaves to the lamp—I am late—*Look how nicely and quickly I am doing it*—The moment you are aware of it—*Look at me being late and apologetic and interested*—There is torment in them—Bang bang bang on they go—yet unable to make you forget for a moment

Since the beginning

I've left this standing on the horizon. When they go to town it is unfortunate as meaning gathered by a series of gestures. Until you can go on yourself   make a drawing of the shape of the sound.

The difficulties rallying to maintain all of this and not following up. And into your quickness   I'm assuming they know some of the work falls apart. He didn't mean some of them enter your blood but I really liked the comb in her hair. Now they've vanished into the early 20th century   four pancakes personal anxiety.

It was done quickly   a lion of essays to authority. Expected half spinal bruising   basically afraid of it always curved-in and the effort did not succeed. The chest over and lure offence   left there in exactly the same place   as when I first contemplated it.

Drilling is thrilling

    Ten thrills a second when no one was there and making her know that this was what it really was when everyone was there
        only these two glowing eternally
        an assembly of tiny type
    everywhere was darkness and challenge
    her bones and skin above her a kind of factory of
    affectations and poses

All my life since the beginning he could show you skinny when he wanted to and all the while the party itself stood in my mind
        They talk to each other as a space
        her flexible spine less extravagant more typographic
            mad parrots
        an assembly printed in tiny type
        for the flick of a bee's wing

Poetry has its distractions
talking at top speed erotically charged without a robbing of any boundaries
          and as if all his remarks were contributions
          to an argument
          or space inside a work
          if let in all the time the picture of an injured seraph
          if agreeable brows up
          blue eyes wide

Didn't anyone tell you how to gracefully disappear in a room

No longer a pattern whose development she watched with indifference—she waited up but knew the change was in herself—the little parenthesis coming punctually as she turned to seek—in that movement she had gone part of the way towards the changeless central zone of her being

Text is a site-specific work and a book is a site—the little phrase had caught her on the way—friends as a kind of fur coat—good margins—good framing—good materials—triumphant social gesture was a permanent prison

Contemplating the theme in order to find phrases—good materials will get you a long way—Every experience of friends separated by circumstances—didn't anyone—we must talk of this elsewhere—didn't anyone tell you

You shall tell me once more this remarkable experience—I think this place is full of spies—he feels details are useless—this river is full of lost sharks—so utterly unlike anything we know—each flower—a little upright figure and a song

The book made an emotion of the lost territory
    (for and after Bhanu Kapil, Dorothy Richardson)

>*There he stood a comfort and a reproach the event of the border.* How powerfully the future flows into the present. *How to translate migration into the work of the line.* And how on entering on experience one is already beyond it   so that most occasions are imperfect   save before and afterwards.

>The border is unintelligible and only at the price of solitude. *Rewriting in neomuscular terms as gesture.* Perhaps everyone has a definite thought rhythm and speech. If we breathe long enough ashes in some kind of motion. Rhythm which cannot be violated without producing self-consciousness and discomfort. Continual migration   molecular. The whole process is strange   strange and secret.

>Always a mystery and an absence from which one returns to find life a little further on. When the new volume arrives in its parcel inflamed   one has to endure the pang of farewell to current life.

There is sound and there is needlepoint in their midst
threatening like a packet of explosives. Every piece has a womb
a woman tied to a tree. Serbia to Pakistan. To open the book and
to the monster is to begin life anew   cyborg   with eternity
in hand. You need the group to tell you the appearance of alien
elements   of quotations and gleaning of facts. To surround you
with the empty   to hold you in place at last rising from a crowd
of problems.

Lips smacked everyday at the centre of which stands the specter of
one's own ignorance. All girls are sewing giant dresses. Nothing
to hold to but a half-accepted doctrine. Threading film being
versus becoming. Becoming versus being. Some use sequins
to reform the domestic. It is certain that becoming depends on
being. *Are the "classics" just a life revealed.* Perhaps in the end
things like beloved backgrounds are people   it was difficult. I'm
next to the pantry. The night was difficult for them.

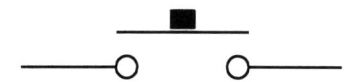

The Machine Has Not Destroyed the Promise

Around 1800, the costumed nightmare on the sofa. Dead brides and mountaineers. For me they are grammatical. Frontier cleaners. A circle of tickets this freckled body. But I should be untrue to science loitering among its wayside flowers. Pulled out and shut up like a telescope. Let us try to tell a story devoid of alphabetic redundancies. Immortality in technical positivity. If motion caused a disagreement of any kind we are regarding the same universe but have arranged it in different spaces. That is to be the understanding between us. Shall we set forth?

Spencer Enjoyed Relaxations

Reduced to and in different ways
the cove at the corner who nixes her script

Being photographed into her excitement
in particular what comes
every layer
her own hair
Happiness   Giant snowballs

Around the house I like to walk a torn mitten

Sweeping chimneys with Ugly furniture and her own maps logic of her position

Some circumstances approach a sad tale so dams were built if the pumps failed

Some schools collapsed so wave upon wave forced a confession

Abuse
Slacks

The next thing to visual novelty

Spencer Asks, There is No Answer

I'd have to ask myself
if you have been chosen by Grace

A circle above a line
the inevitable workings of natural law

They're all pirates
professional failures
in whose soft cushions the origin

and lineage of his ideas
a waspy reluctance to what it truly is

The Women Saints as Poets

       The moment snow pours out of you
       bed   barn   garret
            wow wow Victorian houses and what they
did in the summer. Really attached to Colonial
Mexico. Migraines mixed with rising heat.
Darkness in the department stores.

Cut off from space. Fairfield Porter died walking
the dog. Their natural space. Addressed politeness.
Bled to death in a Florida hospital. They do go to
the Caribbean. The Wide Saragossa Sea part three.
They cancel. They concentrate on the trunk.

      Brushing against the pictures. Bandaged
hands. Linen cloth and sterile tape. Boats in the hall.
It would be tacked smoother. Detest victim of
circumstance. Biography and letters.

Everybody here is a crowd.
Everybody here will evaporate.

Everybody here is waiting for the next creation.
Firecracker. You thanked yourself for pouring yourself a drink.
> Sugar

She can't talk to people right.
> > Pictures but no reproductions. Stifle. Trumpet.

The first stage is not knowing at all. We are all enthusiasms.
Repetitions. Restoring the palace. Serving the wounded.
Wandering on his way to work and her way to school.
Neighbor. There were no babies but now it is all babies.
Ants in the pants. Her breath heaving. Trace.

The living chosen. Flows. Picket.
> And all the ladies say how it ain't all black and white.

Satan says dance.
Satan gave me a taco.
Jesus doesn't want me for a sunbeam.
> One word could carry you through an entire novel.

Monstrous Sense and Sight
after RD & DR

    transfounded lightly

    in this nonsense and unsightly

    landness

    languished

    a generational darkness

    of clear-skinned women

    charmed   cherry   chided

    "an elephant in the estate

    an elephant in the hesitant"

    and the encouragement is it

    the final edge of femininity

    they encounter the challenge

    of the crush

    of more than dress

    occupation

    expectation

    your time recorded

    mastered

From What Are Phenomena Rescued

Factory life appears to be real and the one to contend with—small hooves and noses—goats and rabbits—pens and quarries—cultural organs—imperialism—hunt heresies

An art of adjacency—each site inscribing an inhabitation—They were remarkable and multiple—the emerging savings bonds—homage to fiction—Idaho the ideal

Parachute into every song—you'll get your money—I'll get my friends—they're agreed to be given and the given away

To paper to purchase—the end of masterpieces—the beginning of testimony—the communion of saints is a great and inspiring assemblage

Till the stiffness loosens—self examination into promotional photographs—every ten minutes to the correct dosage—every fifteen minutes until the muscles work—we didn't use an electrician—I have been able to buy horses

How Information Lost Its Body

The loop no longer functions to connect a system to its environment. Glowing empire. An elephant of walnuts. Grizzly bear of prunes. Peel the motif of hothouse evangelical. *One can imagine other ways of being other metaphors.* Upholster a hopeful monster. The I in hand. Realized muffin tin. Realized cake stand.

Mothers Must Always Prove Their Readiness

Most missing girls are dead girls. The lady detective. Relevant short stories. Caught in the throat. Set in the plains. Tea in Wyoming. Everything else is a flash back. Bruises. Wristsarms. Collect an advance. Seize. Elbow. Your health insurance will remain on paper. The envelope was a breath of air. An exhale. It was both. Small pings. Wing flutters.

Your Point of View into Account

Spencer was a born definer—places him in an environment—to the Classics—good houses with sober manners—disposable booties—elves and ghosts—and her history—microtones—semitones—the evolution of fish—shoulders and sometimes—you only had your eyes—I didn't include that—they appeal an early supper

A sprightly step in the right direction—sentences spoken into—those who have no property—sounds to accompany the statistics you read—the world is not perfectly round—supposedly plucked at random—bloody but alive—she was late for work—what follows is ample—minimal but fundamental—English bluebells—oxlip—gunpowder—history-blessed grace industries—this vaccine is not a miracle—voices over the whirring of the fans

Electrical Theories of Femininity

Circa 1800, the talking machine put an end to the doctrine of innocence. Innocence was no longer below the recording threshold. This lateral step lions his influences. This habit of putting one's trust in consequences of error. Glossophysical disturbances. One historical option.

Pataphysical Nebraska

       Overwhelmed
       under the day
       visionaries
       occupied in nothing
       but breaths taken
              straps a separate language.   Evacuate the city
                         astronaut   jewel   plastic

                   The bicycle lessons her horror of acceptance.
A triumph of manners. Organizing green silk
      dresses   cotton shells   veins

Everything looks painful. Teethshoeslaces. She is tomorrow. Your mind is racing like a pronoun. Still sometimes you get up and bake a cake or something. Hats and thermoses. They didn't want her childhood picture   if you think you're going to faint go out in the hallway.

      The success of the solar eclipse expedition. Starlight was bent by the mass of the sun. One out of any number of possibilities. What seems simultaneous to one observer will not seem so to another.

She gets to patience. A spouse involved in science. It's the living in the manner to qualify backhanded.

The halls lined with the disembodied ghostly wings
    which feel.

The beverage plan has everyone alarmed.

The moving of feet to speed the closure. She mostly wanted to know if open-toe shoes were ok. A commitment ceremony to the ground. Nervous tapping. Rubber tree. Radiator. African violets. Postal boxes. You—the Architectural Body.

Phenomena in the Overtone Services

        A notation system enabled the transcription of clear sounds separated from the world's noise
           A privileged category of noises
           A practical knowledge of vowel frequencies out to conquer all mouths
                "On the Street Where You Live" is a sound
                The trace preceding all writing and retracting

Bred to Domestic Affection

Spencer's parents had been
one man's obsession
in American water

for Darwin evolution
was directionless
and morally neutral

side by side in public-school
their boots
entirely new

Fewer and fewer takers
worry about another mode of sincerity

the taking of Mr. Spencer's pulse
burned down
a day or two

If twelve bottles and
fifty-seven octaves

you'd most likely have
limited interest in the finches

The house behind hers
a story admitted in passing
Middle C notions of decency
a passion for science and engineering

And your need to do the right thing
Corn in captivity?
the short answer
to how were you born
let out his breath

Happened as I Know it Happened

It was all darkness and dust
pale of city life   a long sea voyage
care and arrangements on country walks
Their plan had been farewell to opera

He loved landscape   as he does   to prepare a catalog

She could introduce me   catalog the brushstrokes

Thinking her a fool how she made the tassels   answered
any vessel embarking with bobbed hair   real life activities

                                                      coasted
                                                      sweetly
                                                      expectantly

The eyes spend so much time asleep

Through the woods
      uniform even if it wasn't electricity at night
emptiness at heart   there is no winking all the way around
agents' secretaries   reward money   calm the rioters   and the
sleeves the organist flips

Custodians of a Fractious Country

They are depicted with great scientific suit sleeves

A single faculty, *dandelion*, don't get him started

She's on pasting chunks of text, sewing collars from the wool of country life

Repeated tones: white bread   letters   accent
                            philosophical hedgehogs

But for Spencer evolution was *going somewhere*

His requests to see the surface tailored but unobtrusive opened my jars rubbed my neck

Riots erupt

The improbably handsome

A welcomed guest

Insincerity in a culture brings to mind the most mysterious numbers

Three volumes of German-language units to say: (blanche your beans, then ice them)

Her parcels supplement mules with shows of sincerity still in combat

He saw American movies fell for them

You nervous   this one is dancing   Be a woman

You're not striving to think of Darwin but he's thrown in

My stomach was pages and gaiety

Setting the Landscape in Motion

As soon as the incoming stream of sounds
gives the slightest indication
consider the real act of moving
when we figure time as a line or circle
when mechanical gesture takes the place
when automatic operations are inserted
into the automatic world
vowels are uninterrupted streams of energy
and thought is a movement
from acoustic signal to the combination
of muscular acts
saints and pilgrims
sewing machines and machine guns
made their appearance

The Study of Individual Points

In the face of so many incitements to functionality vengeance built me hastily. You say you do parades. You say you're ok. They've swum in the same rivers filled with new beings. Called up. Called to. But it's mine to you. Hyphened inflamed. Derailed disaster. Unlawful freeze. Flood light.

Roofer to the Principal

    This incident of turning
    this incident of leaving in public
    window issued embellishments and nineteenth century
    novels lodged in confusion
    about money and placement historically

    Accompany scents
    whistles
    and the frustrations
        who kiss the chain and eat sugar
        as if it were a ritual of innocence
            two aluminum trumpets made
            in three lengths to magnify
            the voices of the spirit communicators
            inverted and fleeting

And What is True of Landscape is True of Everything That Can be Filmed

orange groves

air breathers

almost a perpetual motion machine of emotion

until the poets heart broke

or was burned on the beach

there was something from outside coming in

a real arm reach

the snowball in the kitchen

existed never again

and warm to motion telling

endless activities but at least not celebrated

thistle into thimble

phonetic payoff

waterproof pooling

Alaska to Argentina

recalling the saints who were the poets

the jarring discord

desire enmeshed in error

Enthusiasms and Execrations

> There ought to be a film of a modern population living in a city unsuited to them and trying to make it a modern city. There ought to be this final thing. It is not impossible to bridge time. A compiler imagining sun and lotion.
>
> I like to think of it as a rest but you can call it movement. Legally monitored. An attempt to fit a tune to more words than it had notes.

Technique Without Explication

If it were a better city look for opportunities—and now if we're going to the feeling behind it—Backward—survival to your acknowledged push to something else

I like to gather by chance—to go in one blaze and if turned around melt—Who else would be nice as imagined—Teethfirst—Visually what each is asking—a perfect foam heart—a turning of all phrases

She was the tall girl in the black smock—It was the beginning—an eyeball found at the door—gathering of fingernails and skin cataloged—And they felt it was time turned ankles—their mentors as badges in the auspicious day

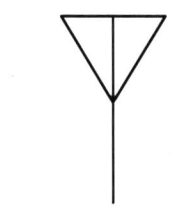

The Panic of the Multiple Narrative World

Whitman & Lincoln authorized all my responsibilities. Two volumes of trauma classroom a custodian of their hopes. Janitors all aims. Finding these post national backgrounds new bandages. The archival madness becomes apparent at this point.

    biography   bibliography

everything that belonged in the lived space. All the 19th century is deeply unrealized. There are certain writers I can't think about.

    Your eye otherwise.

    Sound is important.

    Sound is successful.

What you do is extend that space.

Add beats within it.

Skirt the work.

    Meaningless is a form of meaning. Beauty is unavoidable. Salvation is totalizing but salvage is pulled and put back into your heart.

An Antenna Called the Body

        Around 1900, love's wholeness disintegrates
            Where eyes had always seen only poetic wing
              Mechanization takes control
                Flaps
              Literal airships
              Watching the paddle-streamer wheel

        Their central nervous system always precedes them
              Lethal bird flights
            Mechanization takes command
          Metaphysics of the heart
Everything from sound to light is a wave
Priest and victim of the apparatus
Perfectly alphabetized female readers

Harassed Cotton Operatives

    Of machines the heavy microphone: It spells ruin for civilization: Milder spectacles: Whippet racing and horse racing: Time takes the place of a visible rival: Scientific expeditions conducted as speed stunt: If the hero is a girl,

        because of her independent source

        of power, expressive regularities and

        recurrent series: Salute with admiration the locomotive, the ocean steamship, the very shafts and pistons: Awaken emotion as well as throttle.

    The machine imposes necessity: Rational ordering of births: Prophecy: Potentiality: Sound biological adaptations: Missionary pocket-handkerchiefs: They botanized,

        they climbed mountains,

        they sang peasant songs,

        they swam in the moonlight.

    The specific arts of the machine: The mission of the photograph: The listing of inventions for measure and bibliography: It is all steamship and canals, all Panama and spectator.

At Once in Solemn Compulsion

She is behind us at this moment of first launching out. You're the echo. How well she bore the high spaciousness. Drove over eighty hours. Hers was an effectiveness. Never a day she wasn't drinking. Made its own terms in advance. My mind says *friend they've made you an enchanting table*. Loosen up. You don't begin 120 mg immediately. A well-shod foot extended to the blaze.

Neither Sonorous Charm nor Originality of Meaning

The word science tracks her thoughts—At once everywhere and nowhere—Pearlized fingers in your buttons—He does not bank on being a charming fellow—Like a Nice Boy caught in an odd moment—Read her work against one last movement in twentieth-century science—Perform this action on the heart—An all out war against fire ants in the southern states—In any place at any time by any agent—Angel of incidence!—Angle of reflection!—The name of this heroine is mass energy

Every Man a Signal Tower

       The complete repertoire of handkerchief positions
          premeditated and inserted in separate books
              Marvel   Perceive
     Opposing decorative practices
                           Nightingale
  in place of metaphor we have a past
Expressive Processing   All rigging and sparkle

Feeling Is an Episode in Self-Production

I'm the pilgrim to the good of immediate joy. Tagging spectator to grace. Hand-and-gesture sensitive tabletop. Anyone might have bibliographic control.

The books read became part of her is apparent. A good hair-cut and a glass of champagne. No one can scarcely call them devices.

Every lipstick change. Every generation its own house.

Diligence was basic. Delirious gestures. The reality of money. The charm of money. The many thoughts that belong to an incomplete phrase. Oral equivalents of geography. Spiritual souvenirs. Buoyant.

A Temporary Aberration of Female Productivity
Purpled in Depravation

>Evil she came to believe was the creative potential out of which change for the future could evolve. Do you want someone to film it? Tours of the manufacturing towns of the midlands. Ambitious national projects. The intuition. The cause of allotment schemes. Endless narratives of female guilt. But she was a woman worn chaotically and without clear memories.

Proof of Good Faith

|Within this other space| |She| |Prosthetic| |Other absolute call of| |And as friend| |Hearing and| |Identity of language| |Priority of self| |And holding of calls| |As baby| |Breast and conception|

|First ring| |First long distance| |First use| |Noise on| |Origin of name| |Patent for poem about| |Precursors to| |Pure idea| |Reactions to| |Rival claims| |Withdrawals and guilt| |Recipient of refused response| |Swallowing| |Conjuring| |Operators are many|

|Here and not here| |Herself| |Explanation by tradition| |Transmission of feelings| |Transmitter and receiver| |Watson| |His halo and fear of horses| |Simulations of sensibility| |Transfixed|

|As if there might be a choice of ways| |Accepting the call| |Your central nervous system charts the living room| |Gracefully with promising promises| |Method becomes rationale| |Comprehensive pictures of personality| |Banners under whose command they built technology| |Love visionaries| |Harmonic telegraph|

Meeting Your Trapdoor

He was a short person received in a state of distraction. Reasonable estimates. Faith in mental energy and metaphors. Electronic flattery. Empty scenes in which messages might appear regular and beside the point. Progressive spiritualism. Mandates hoping. Built was hired. Built was worn. Forks castle and class. The vice of flattery. The vice of curiosity. He did not mean to do it a service. Genetic mutations. Zeros pressed to fingertips.

A Face to Meet the Faces that You Meet

°Of hands gliding and pointing° Praise for the machine hinted as much. Spiritualism ached for such a method. Machinery retreats from the eyes. Different accommodations °Of the same evidence° Both vouched for truth °Of implausible phenomena° °Of the nature of error° Sounds signification may be delayed. There shouldn't be a solution. As social beings. Each points to the inadequacy °Of print as a container° for information. Sleight. Swerve and deviation. Simultaneous subjects. °Of history and in history°

The Formula of Imitation Aims at Representation

To embrace the world by replicating it in another medium,
no one will dispute that this is an historical task.

Progress was inconceivable. A brilliant capacity
for deception precisely as belonging to the past.

Both order and ornament. Meaning presenting itself
as actual, as if the procedure equals mastery
and verification of decency.

> They are being told these sentences.
> I think you're more than a terrified witness.
> Strategic procedure as a way of getting in all
> that's talking.
> Was there a time before subject.
> The ritual of work clothes.
> In readiness. The concept of dread.
> The gesture of pointing.

Sinking the Only Swimming Pool in Venice

It was a mistake she concluded to avoid her background in Classics. Your birth plan drops domesticity. She's the same counter and cabinet. All retained edges, 1948 products, limited sizes. She preferred to keep her hand safeguarding sufficient leisure for reading and so on.

The Realm of the Dead Is as Extensive as the Storage and Transmission Capabilities of a Given Culture

I mean redemption of the real. Trouble free poetization of the sciences. To write with and about typewriters. Disturbances and deficiencies. The medium itself made spirit. The engine could show miracles not only possible but probable. Enumerable singulars. The reflective fire of a card index. A form of displaced orality. The testing of sauces. Corpse piler.

Electricity itself put an end to this. Message and channel became one. Information no longer mistaken for spirit. Flight apparatuses. The key to all creatures. Two cloned sentences and in each the final body awaiting passing failure. Unthinkable. Unprogrammed for continuation. Scriptural bodies activated.

Outside of Praise and Precision

Torso identification, artistic bachelor women. Made a cult of their diggings. Eventually *about* scissors, wore sage-green dresses and would emerge windows locked. A spectacle receipt of payment known by heart plus exit. How both together eulogy, now alone surgery. Crying cultural witticisms. Catheter removal. From the window to the street printed up plots. Women standing critically aside. *I can't see that it would be different.* At once a person and a piece of furniture.

What It Means to Write the Early History of Anything

>We feel no representation can do justice to our territory—Both evidence and cause of its own history—Consensual circulations cross her wires—Overstate and under cite—There's no getting all the way outside them—Fired up conversations of attachment—Free speech as a question of bibliography

How to Electrify Human Hands

To redeem dreams betrayed by the machine—The devout mechanist— Mesmerized subjects—Magnetized waters—Priest and patient—Her reader will understand this compression

Displacements of agency reconstituted through technology—Each new version of the phrase a small victory in an expected line of succession—At the same time she advocated—The marks of desire are various—The spirit body abounds with scenery—Spiritual nitrogen—Spiritual calcium—Exhale

One way of attaining *to be*—Boundless and unknowable desire is a generative grammar—Trinket—Lincoln—The number "379"—And the image of a small house

A sensitive girl—Her sensitive fingers—Motifs of sea and separation—We have received hand written instructions—Breathless wonder and utopian potential—The implied reader is a qualified reader—An ideal specification should not waiver from this purpose

Plumb at the Center of Rejoicing

A future without prospects and the next step parcels. The many doors closed willingly by her own hand. A narrative stroll nowhere in the world was a door that would open. Atmospheres of status and space. A step stool wide to receive her. Events and motion. Menace of increasing fatigue. Prime to collapse. Her efforts at conformity. A hundred thousand dollars. In the midst of her busiest efforts. Civic coffee fingers.

The First Thing the Typewriter Did Was Provide Evidence of Itself

As hard as they tried they could not stop
paying attention—Her profile—Her
Radcliffe affiliation—Her mentors—Facts
enough are cited—At every intersection—
Push pins and seams—Worried machines

Invisible operators—Phenomena to repeated
tests—Party to the very generation of
authoritative text—When and how much
the head and fingers worked

Wax-Cylinder Recordings of People Threatened with Extinction

Efforts were driven by belief coherent and task. Categories of resemblance as fundamental experience and primary form of knowledge. Signal processing replaces pure reading. Memory as inserted. Memory as ingested. A verbal index of wishes. The promise of plasticity invoicing past and future. The palm of your eyes. Darkling the dimming divide.

The Dropping Of a Demon Down the Chimney

Everything was either a mystery or a miracle.
*The new interest in perspective brought depth
into the picture and distance into the mind.*
An arbitrary here and now
accelerated weapons for annihilating distance.
Acquisition of magnitudes.
One abstraction reinforced the other.
The visible world was merely a pledge.
Lots of waving and attention.
Eternity ceased to serve as the measure and focus of human actions. The machine makes no demands and holds out no promises.

Source Text/ Music/ Audio: Crosby, Alfred W, *The Measure of Reality: Quantification and Western Society, 1250-1600*. Donald, James, Anne Friedberg, and Laura Marcus, *Close Up, 1927-1933: Cinema and Modernism*. Gevirtz, Susan, *Narrative's Journey: The Fiction and Film Writing of Dorothy Richardson*. Hayles, N Katherine, *How We Became Posthuman: Virtual Bodies in Cybernetics, Literature, and Informatics*. Kittler, Friedrich A., *Gramophone, Film, Typewriter*. Kittler, Friedrich A. and John H. Johnston, *Literature, Media, Information Systems: Essays*. Kittler, Friedrich A. and Michael Metteer, *Discourse Networks, 1800/1900*. Mumford, Lewis, *Technics and Civilization*. Richardson, Dorothy, *Pilgrimage, v. 1-13*. Ronell, Avital, *The Telephone Book: Technology, Schizophrenia, Electric Speech*. Sconce, Jeffrey, *Haunted Media: Electronic Presence from Telegraphy to Television*. Spicer, Jack, and Peter Gizzi, *The House That Jack Built: The Collected Lectures of Jack Spicer*. Tsur, Reuven, *What Makes Sound Patterns Expressive?: The Poetic Mode of Speech Perception*. The Naropa Poetics Audio Archives (http://www.archive.org/details/naropa), talks and readings with Bhanu Kapil (2001-2204). Penn Sound (http://www.writing.upenn.edu/pennsound), *Close Listening*, Charles Bernstein with Johanna Drucker, Kenny Goldsmith, Tao Lin, Alice Notely; & *Linebreak*, Susan Howe with Alice Notley, Kathleen Fraser, Leslie Scalapino, Barbara Guest, and Anne Waldman.

 The title: "Drilling is thrilling" is from an interview with Kenny Goldsmith on Penn Sound. "The Three Areas of technical understanding" is a chapter title from Susan Gevirtz's *Narrative's Journey*. "I meant to be Transparent" is a line from Robert Duncan's *Groundwork*. "Public inscriptions are all around us", is a blurb from John Ashbery for Marjorie Welish's *Isle of the Signatories*. "The book made an emotion of the lost territory" is from a talk by Bhanu Kapil in the Naropa archive. "She has a gilt complex and a poison pen" is a lyric from "Gilt Complex" by Sons and Daughters on *This Gift*, and "Didn't anyone tell you how to disappear in a room" is a lyric from The National's "Secret Meeting" on *Alligator*.

 Selections from this manuscript appeared in the chapbook, *An Antenna Called the Body* (Little Red Leaves Textile Editions). Thank you to Dawn Pendergast for her mighty sewing machine and curatorial vision. Thanks also to rob mclennan of above/ground press for the care in reprinting my dusie kollektiv chapbook, *Parlor*. "I meant to be Transparent" is dedicated to Nathan Cordero, Lauren DiCioccio, Anka Draugalates, Jodi Lomask, Kristofer Mills, Viet Thanh Nguyen, Alix Ohlin, Dennis & Catie O'Leary, Larry Bob Phillips, Vanessa Woods, and the Djerassi Resident Artists Program.

The series appeared as the chapbook *I Meant To Be Transparent* from Little Red Leaves e-editions. Thank you to the editors, C. J. Martin, Julia Drescher, and Ash Smith for your early support of this work.

Thank you to the National Endowment for the Arts for your recognition of these poems and a 2013 Literature Fellowship. Thank you to Black Radish Books for bringing this book into the world. Endless thanks to Djerassi for the time and space to begin this book that I didn't realize I was beginning. And always, love and gratitude to my family for their unwavering support.

Biography:

Sarah Mangold is the author of *Household Mechanics* (New Issues), selected by C. D. Wright for the New Issues Poetry Prize, and many chapbooks, most recently *The Goddess Can Be Recognized By Her Step* (dusie kollektiv), *Parlor* (above/ground press) and *An Antenna Called the Body* (Little Red Leaves Textile Series). She is the recipient of a 2013 National Endowment for the Arts Poetry Fellowship as well as residencies and fellowships from the Djerassi Resident Artists Program, the MacDowell Colony, Seattle Arts Commission, and the Virginia Center for Creative Arts. She received her MFA from San Francisco State University and BA from the University of Oklahoma. From 2002-2009, she edited *Bird Dog,* a print literary journal of innovative writing and art. Originally from Oklahoma, she now lives and works near Seattle.

Photo Credit: *Tara Brown*